Big Mouths

Written by Jo Windsor

This bird has
a big mouth.

pelican

3

This hippo has a big mouth.

hippo

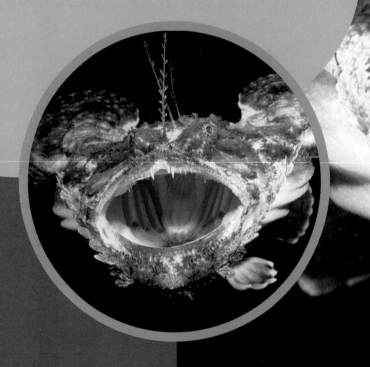

This fish has
a big mouth.

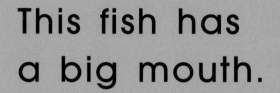

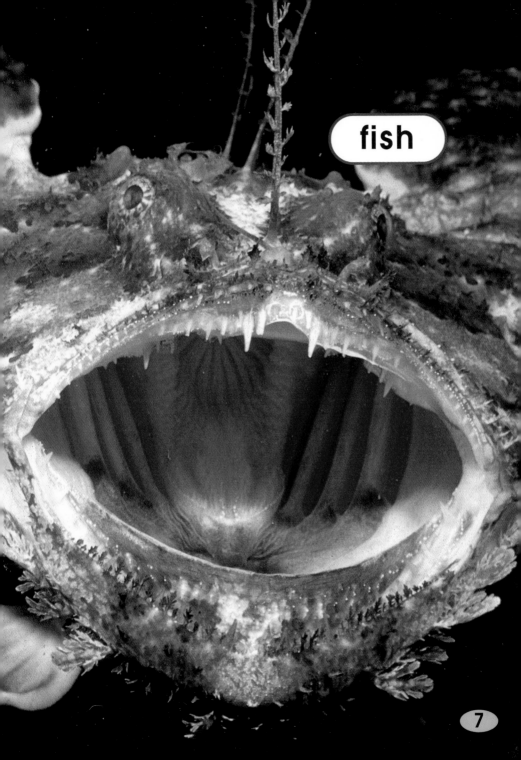

fish

7

This crocodile has a big mouth.

crocodile

This shark has a big mouth.

shark

This whale has
a big, big mouth.

whale

Index

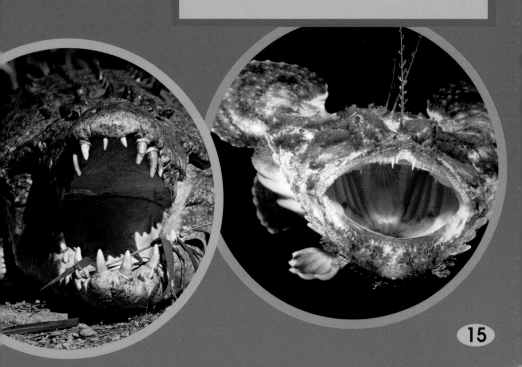

Guide Notes

Title: Big Mouths

Stage: Emergent – Magenta

Genre: Nonfiction (Expository)

Approach: Guided Reading

Processes: Thinking Critically, Exploring Language, Processing Information

Written and Visual Focus: Photographs (static images), Index, Labels

FORMING THE FOUNDATION

Tell the children that this book is about animals that have big mouths.
Talk to the children about what is on the front cover. Read the title and the author.
Focus the children's attention on the index and talk about the animals that are
in this book.
"Walk" through the book, focusing on the photographs and talk about the animals that
have big mouths and why they might have big mouths.

Read the text together.

THINKING CRITICALLY

(sample questions)

After the reading
* Why do you think some animals have big mouths?
* What animal do you think has the biggest mouth?

EXPLORING LANGUAGE

(ideas for selection)

Terminology
Title, cover, author, photographs

Vocabulary
Interest words: bird, fish, shark, whale
High-frequency words: this, has, a